'TWAS THE NIGHT BEFORE CHRISTMAS

Manufactured in USA.

8 7 6 5 4 3 2 1

ISBN 1-56173-724-0

Contributing writer: Carolyn Quattrocki

Cover illustration: Linda Graves

Book illustrations: Susan Spellman

Publications International, Ltd.

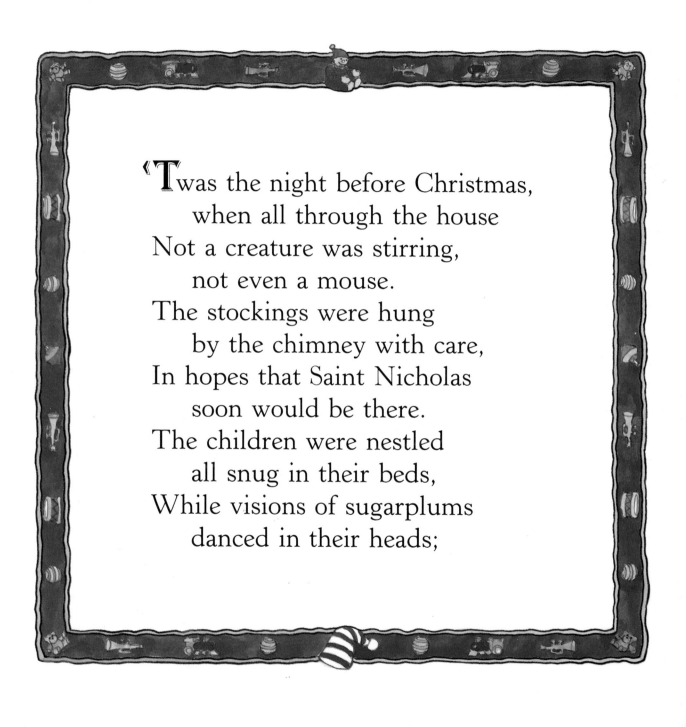

'Twas the night before Christmas,
    when all through the house
Not a creature was stirring,
    not even a mouse.
The stockings were hung
    by the chimney with care,
In hopes that Saint Nicholas
    soon would be there.
The children were nestled
    all snug in their beds,
While visions of sugarplums
    danced in their heads;

And mamma in her kerchief,
    and I in my cap,
Had just settled our brains
    for a long winter's nap—
When out on the lawn
    there arose such a clatter
I sprang from my bed
    to see what was the matter.
Away to the window
    I flew like a flash,
Tore open the shutter,
    and threw up the sash.

The moon on the breast
    of the new-fallen snow
Gave a luster of midday
    to objects below;
When what to my
    wondering eyes should appear
But a miniature sleigh
    and eight tiny reindeer,
With a little old driver,
    so lively and quick,
I knew in a moment
    it must be Saint Nick!

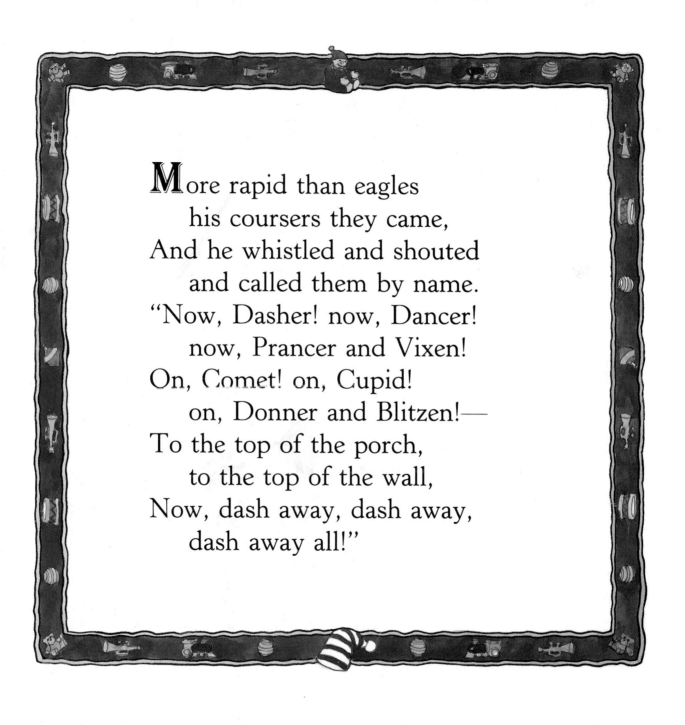

More rapid than eagles
    his coursers they came,
And he whistled and shouted
    and called them by name.
"Now, Dasher! now, Dancer!
    now, Prancer and Vixen!
On, Comet! on, Cupid!
    on, Donner and Blitzen!—
To the top of the porch,
    to the top of the wall,
Now, dash away, dash away,
    dash away all!"